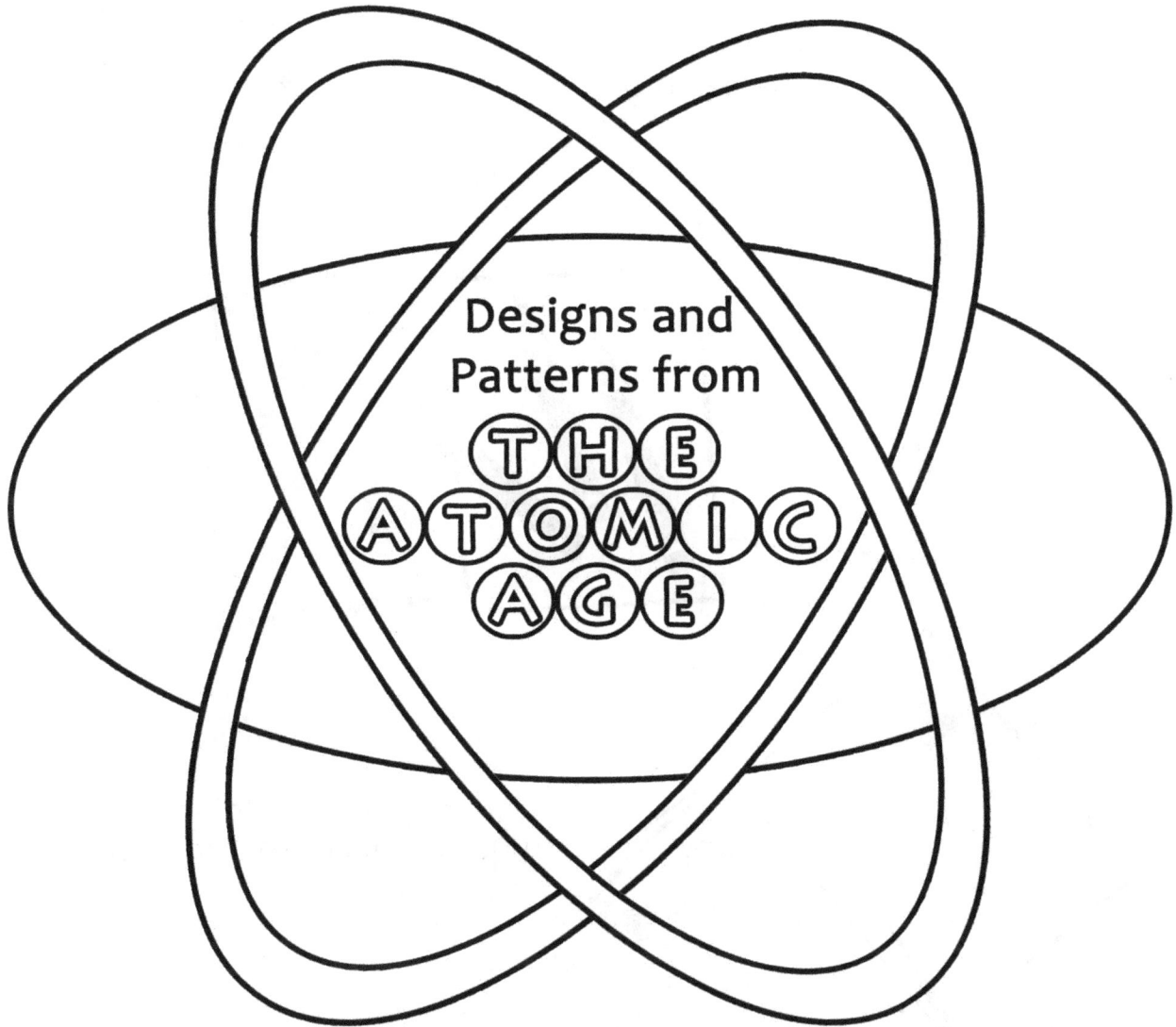

Designs and Patterns from

THE ATOMIC AGE

Artwork by Kate Harper

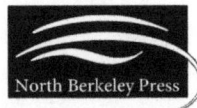

North Berkeley Press

North Berkeley Press1715 Eola Street, Berkeley CA 94703

ISBN-13: 978-0692635339
ISBN-10: 0692635335

Coloring Tips:

Place a blank sheet of paper
under the page you are going to color.

When you are finished,
you can cut out the page.

Hang it up on a bulletin board
for others to enjoy!

North Berkeley Press

www.kateharperdesigns.com

North Berkeley Press

www.kateharperdesigns.com

North Berkeley Press

www.kateharperdesigns.com

North Berkeley Press

www.kateharperdesigns.com

North Berkeley Press

www.kateharperdesigns.com

North Berkeley Press

www.kateharperdesigns.com

North Berkeley Press

www.kateharperdesigns.com

North Berkeley Press

www.katharperdesigns.com

North Berkeley Press

www.kateharperdesigns.com

North Berkeley Press

www.kateharperdesigns.com

North Berkeley Press

www.kateharperdesigns.com

North Berkeley Press

www.katcharperdesigns.com

North Berkeley Press

www.kateharperdesigns.com

North Berkeley Press

www.kateharperdesigns.com

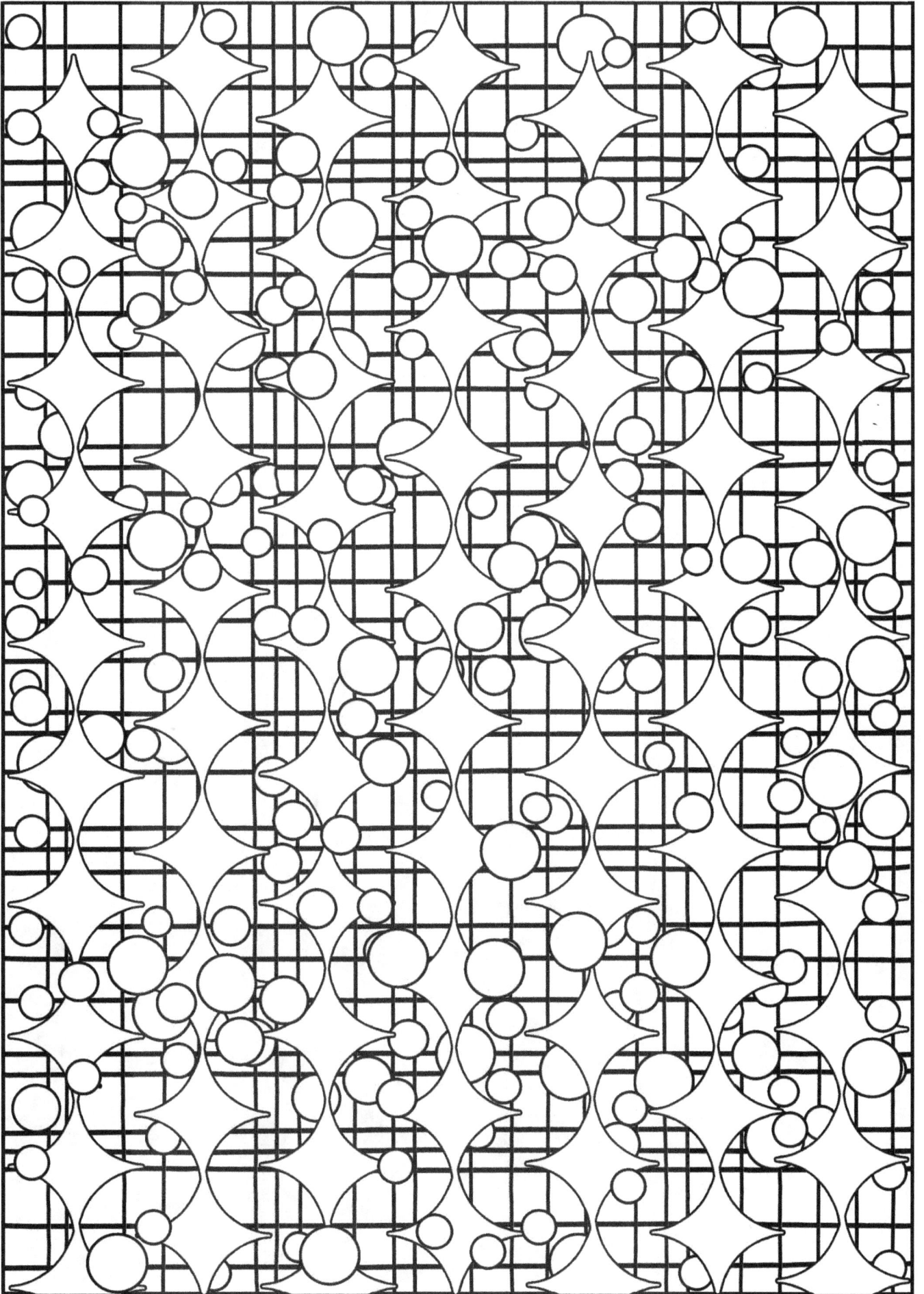

North Berkeley Press

www.kateharperdesigns.com

North Berkeley Press

www.katharperdesigns.com

North Berkeley Press

www.kateharperdesigns.com

North Berkeley Press

www.kateharperdesigns.com

North Berkeley Press

www.katcharperdesigns.com

THE ATOMIC AGE

North Berkeley Press

www.kateharperdesigns.com

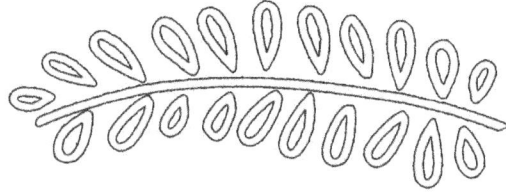

Stationery

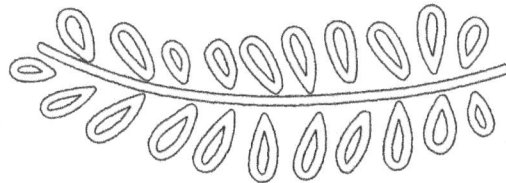

Color your own decorative envelopes with matching stationery.

Guidelines:

- Color your stationery page and envelope before cutting.
- Cut out along along dotted lines.
- To assemble your envelope, fold on solid lines.
- Glue both side flaps.
- After envelope is dry, insert folded stationery sheet.

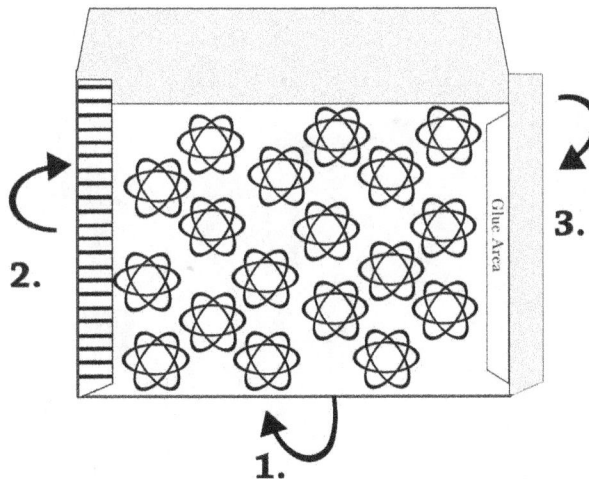

Glue Area

2.

3.

1.

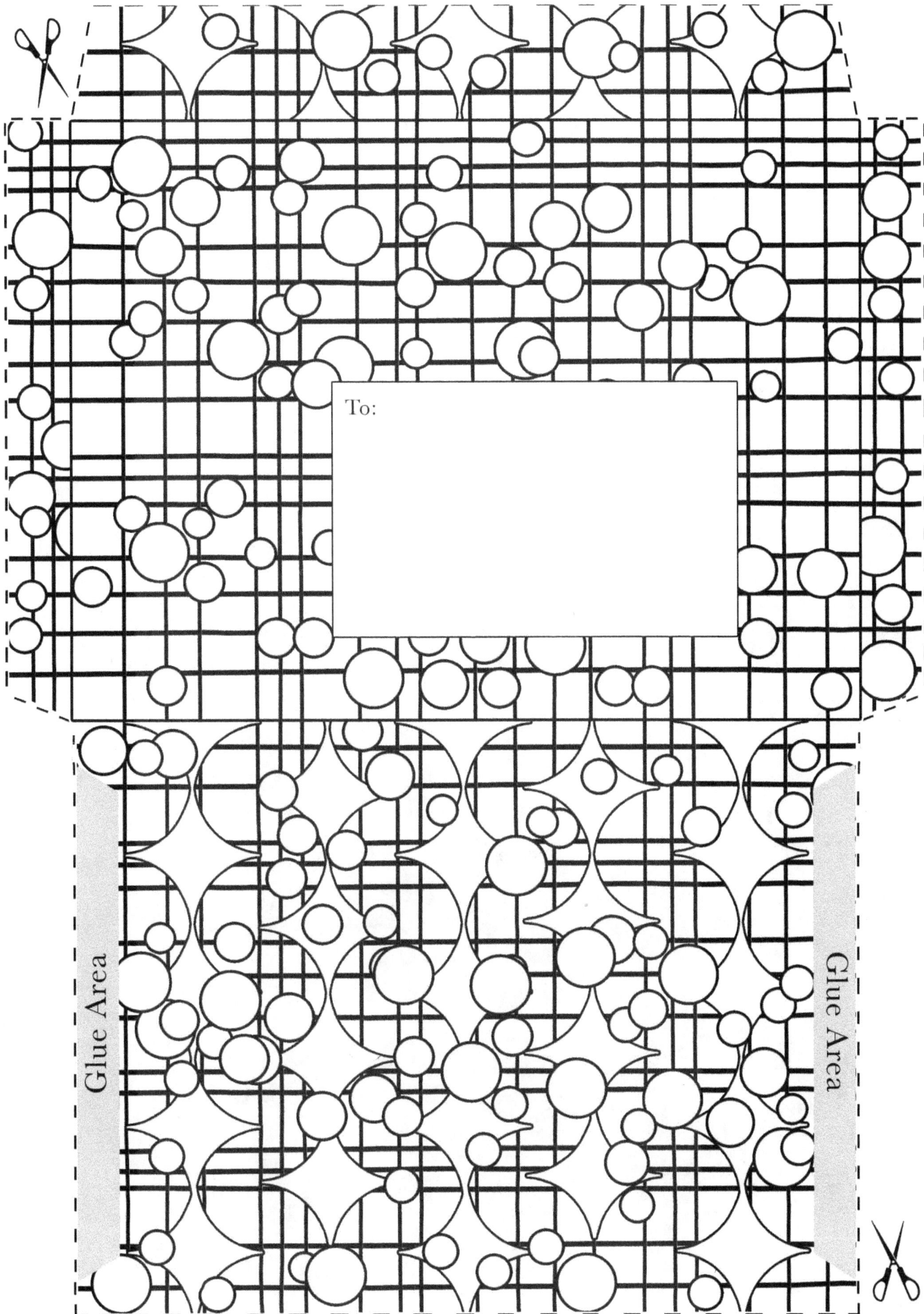

To:

Glue Area

Glue Area

To:

To:

To:

Glue Area

Glue Area

To:

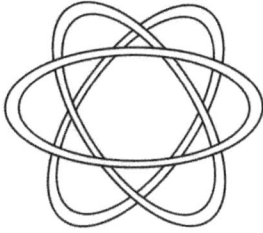

To:

To:

Glue Area

Glue Area

To:

Glue Area

Glue Area

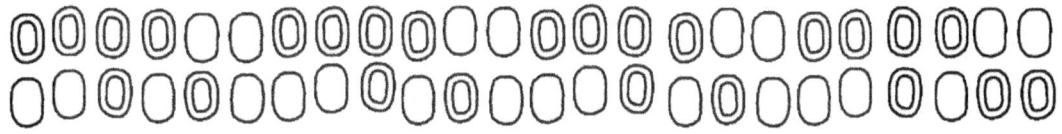

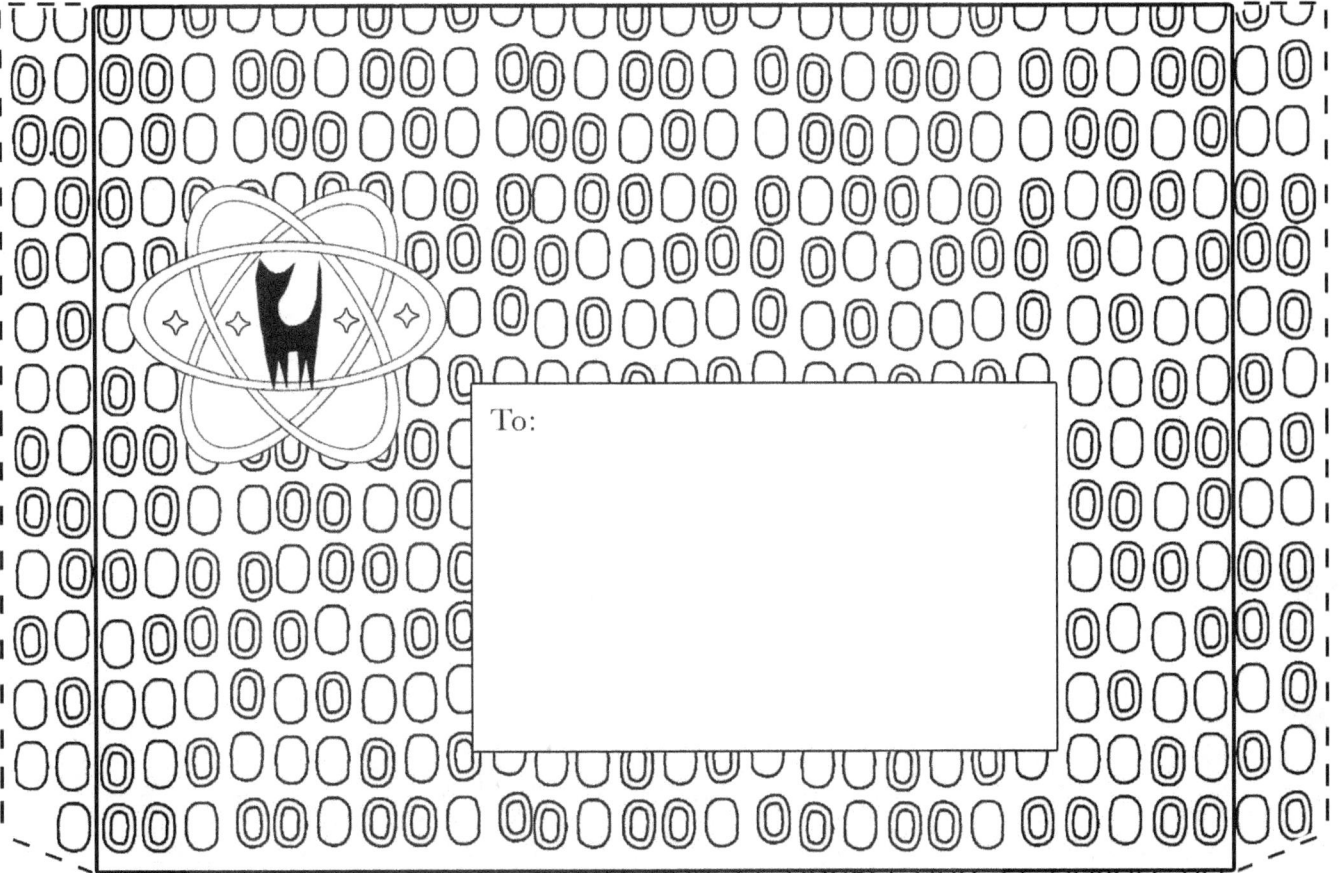

To:

Glue Area

Glue Area

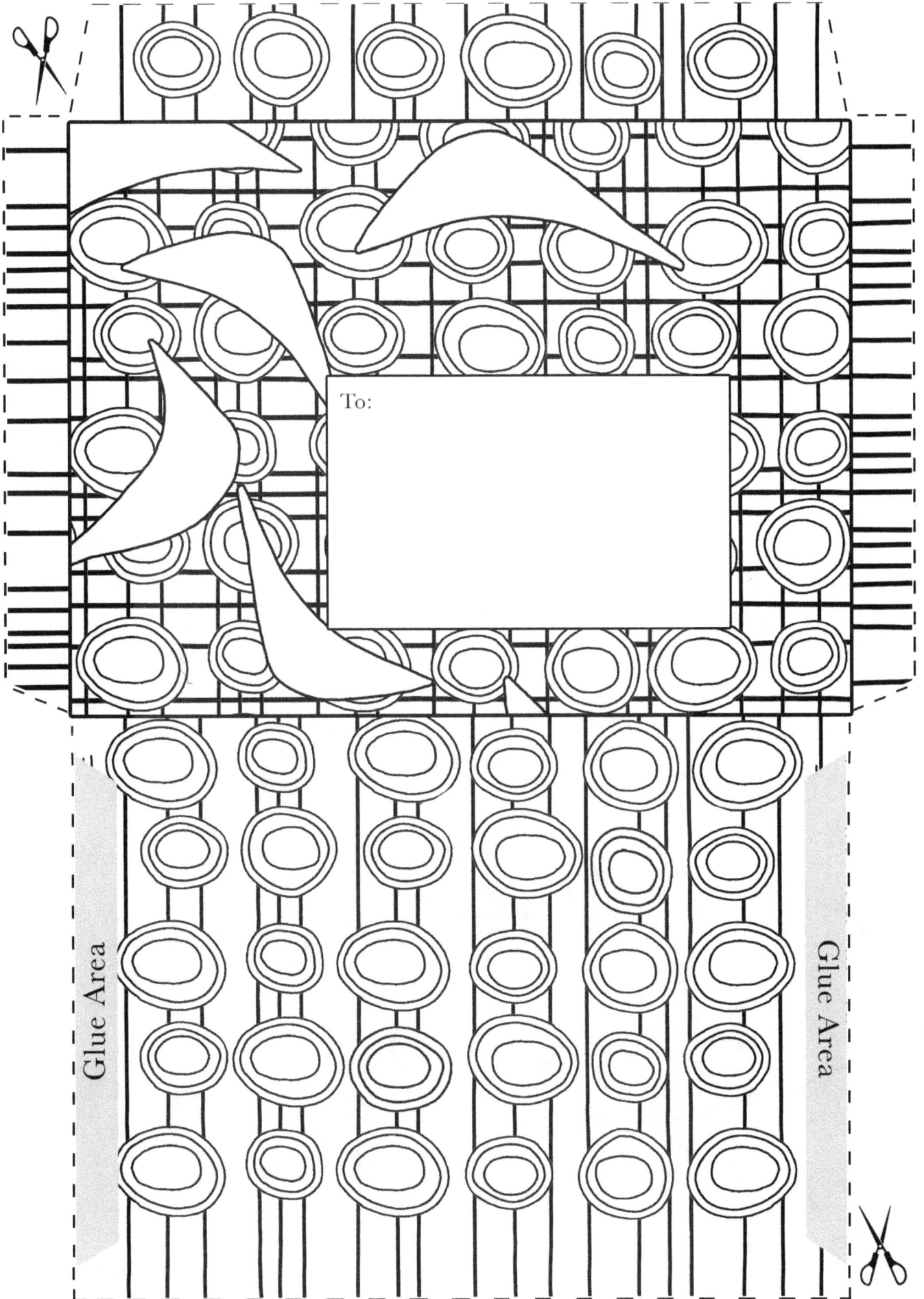

To:

Glue Area

Glue Area

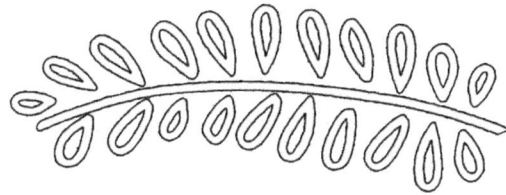

Frameables

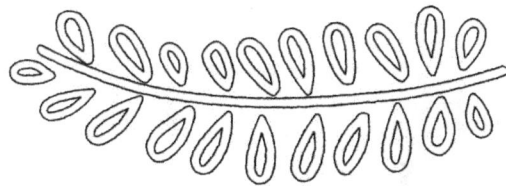

Frameables are smaller versions of the large coloring pages.
These images fit a 4 1/2 x 6 inch photo frame
and are ideal for a fun gift.

THE ATOMIC AGE

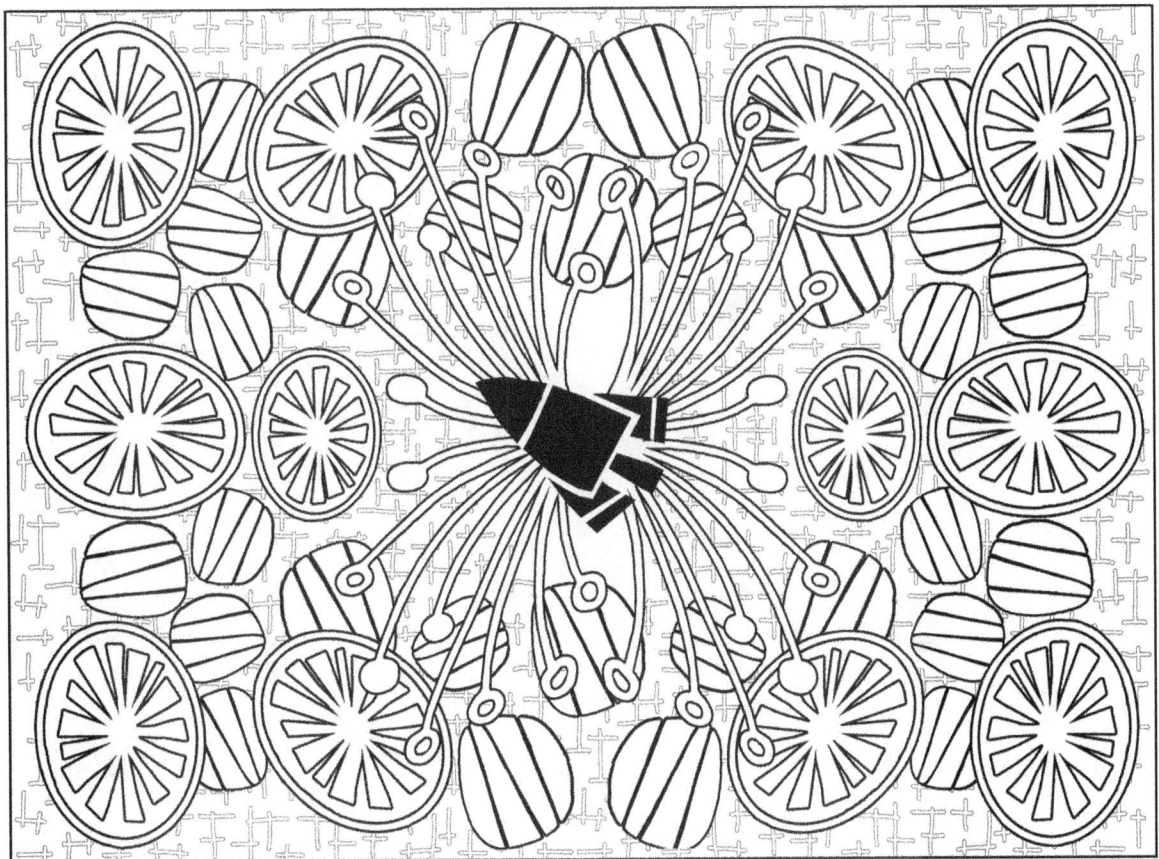

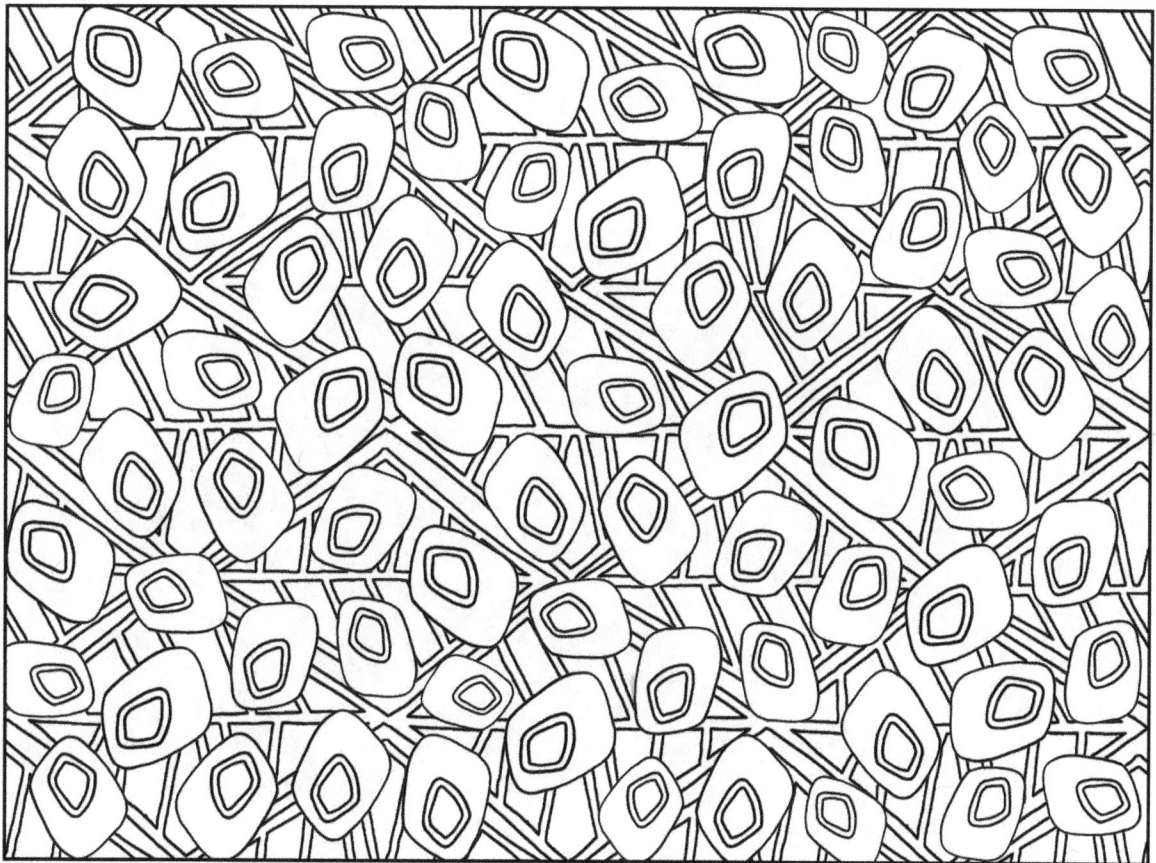

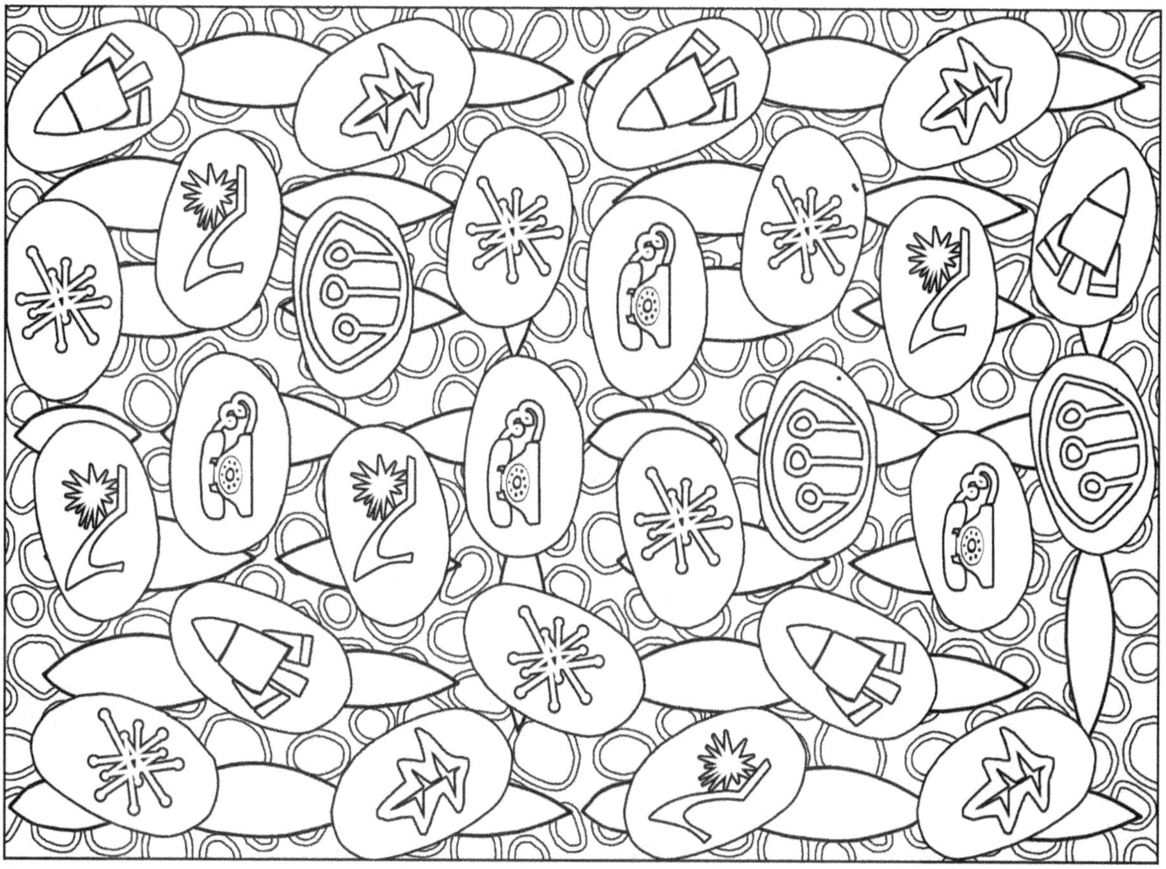

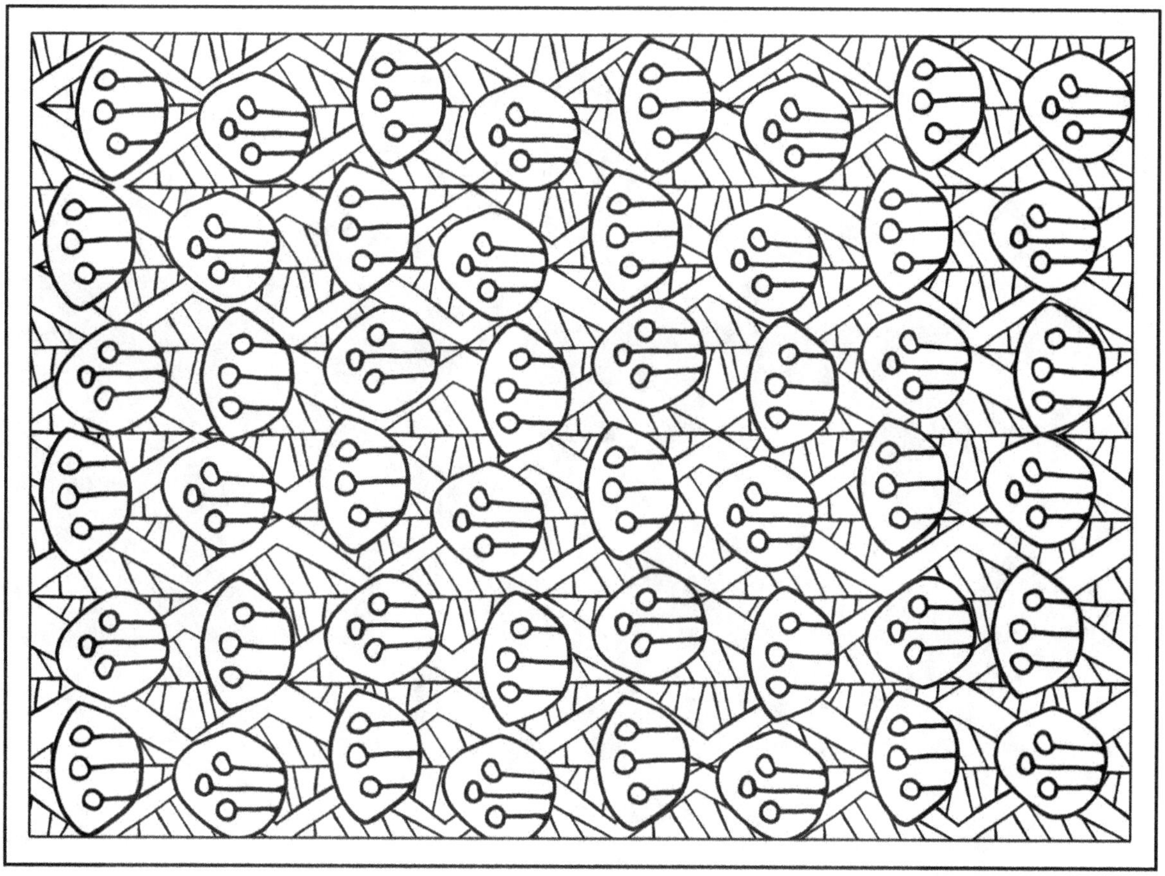

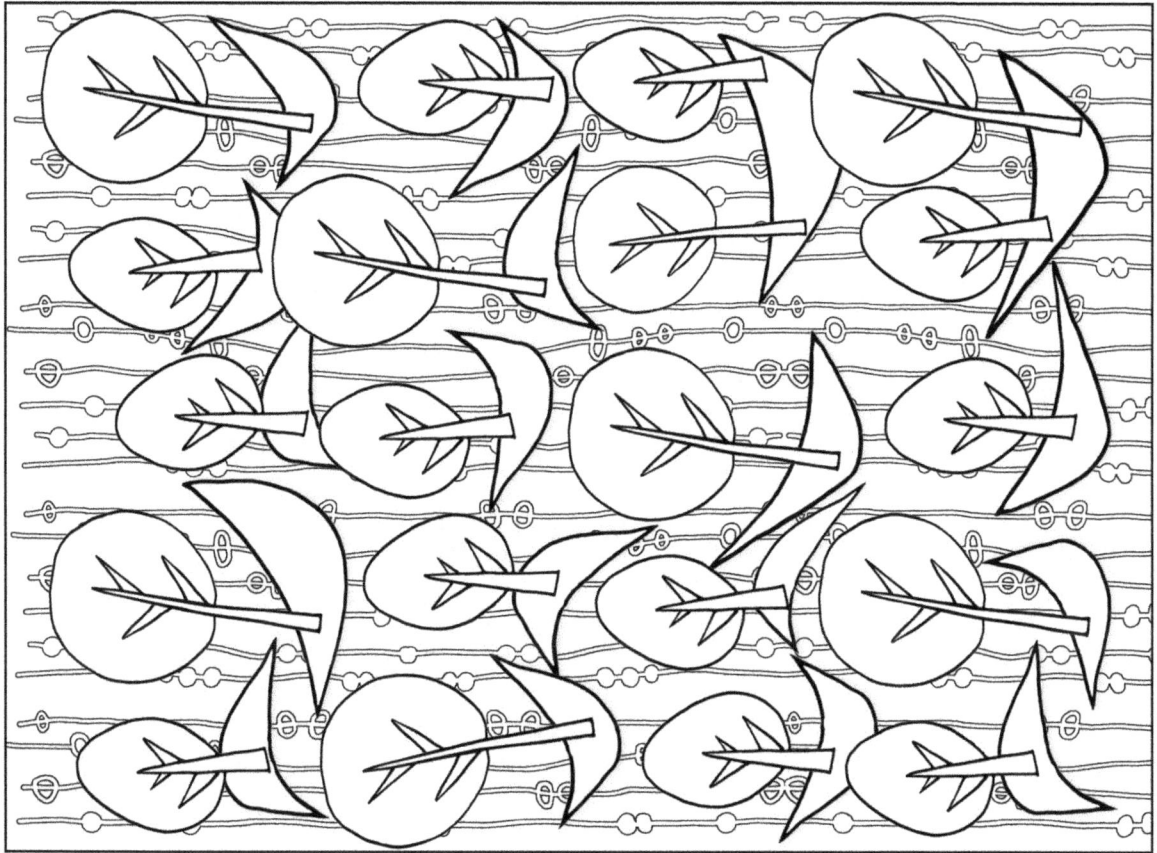

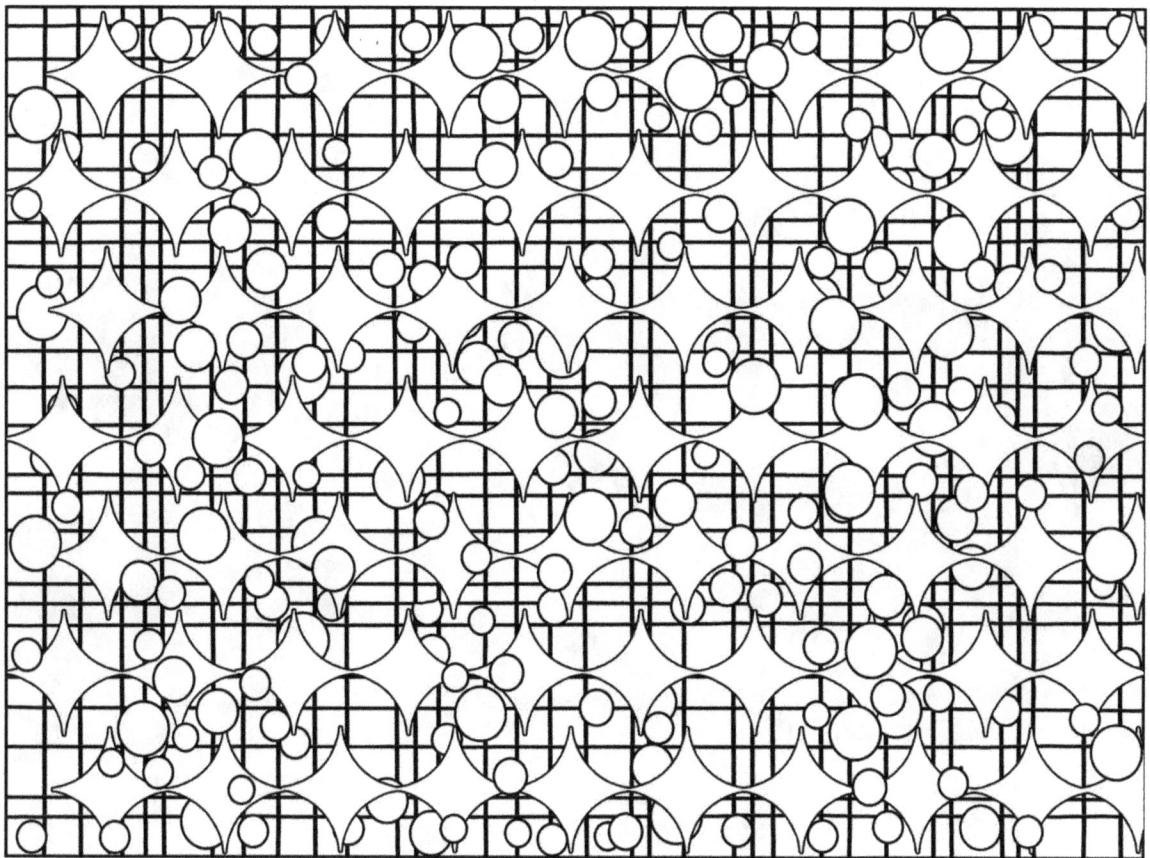

ABOUT THE AUTHOR

Kate Harper is a greeting card and gift designer in Berkeley, California.
She is also an adult education instructor and has taught a variety
of art classes throughout the San Francisco bay area.

Kate has a B.A. in Art Therapy from Indiana University
and an M.A. in Expressive Therapies from Lesley University,
in Cambridge Massachusetts.

~

Free Coloring Pages
Kate would love to hear from you at kateharp@aol.com
Send your feedback and suggestions, or post a review on Amazon.
You will receive free coloring pages that are guaranteed to make you laugh.

Website
www.kateharperdesigns.com

Facebook page:
https://www.facebook.com/kateharperdesigns/

Other Books by Kate Harper
To see more publications by Kate, visit her author page on Amazon.com at:
amazon.com/author/kateharper

North Berkeley Press

www.kateharperdesigns.com

Patterns from the Atomic Age

Designs and Patterns from the Atomic Age

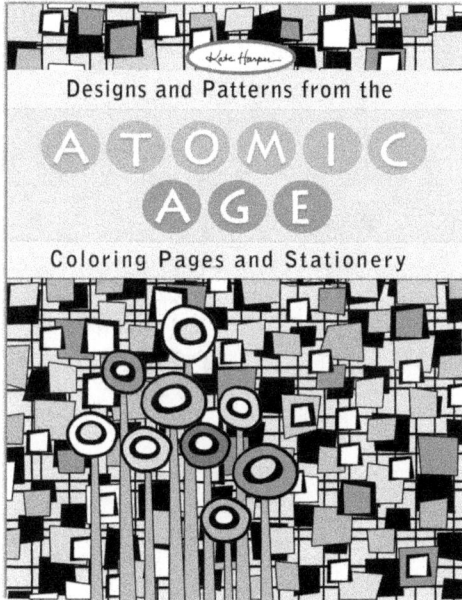

This book will let you time travel to the Atomic Age of design. In the 50's and 60's these irregular shapes and patterns represented hope on the forefront of a new era of technology. Later, they evoked a calming sense of longing and nostalgia for simpler times. Maybe you saw these themes featured on TV shows, propaganda films, and the various stylings from the Fallout franchise. These mid-century modern designs have delighted Americans during some of the most tense chapters of our history.

Modern life is full of pressures and stresses. Today, we face decisions and doubts that our forebears did not confront. These happy and cheerful patterns can be a retreat to calm and center yourself. A perfect coloring book the whole nuclear family.

Coloring Pages

Stationery and Envelopes

North Berkeley Press

www.kateharperdesigns.com

Divorce and Breakup Coloring Book

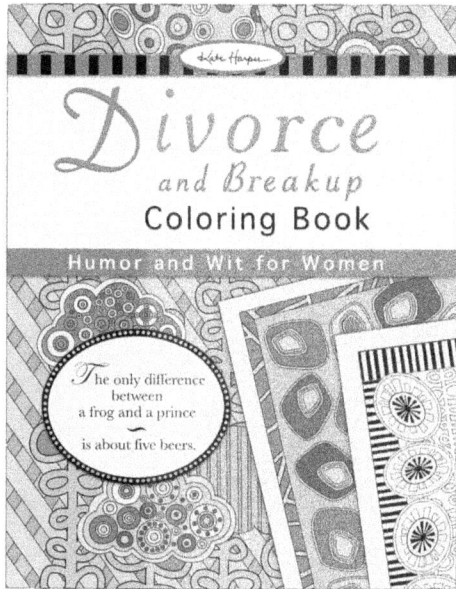

Kate Harper

Divorce
and Breakup
Coloring Book

Humor and Wit for Women

The only difference between a frog and a prince is about five beers.

If you are a woman who has been through a divorce, or perhaps you are going through a breakup, this coloring book will help you keep a smile on your face through all the ups and downs.

Full of uplifting designs, original patterns, and lighthearted quotes, this book can help you get your groove back!

Don't get mad. Get new shoes.

I kissed the frog.

I married the prince.

I divorced the toad.

Men are like airplanes. Expect delays, cancellations, and a lot of turbulence, before you make the right connection.

North Berkeley Press

www.kateharperdesigns.com

Ebooks by Kate Harper

amazon.com/author/kateharper

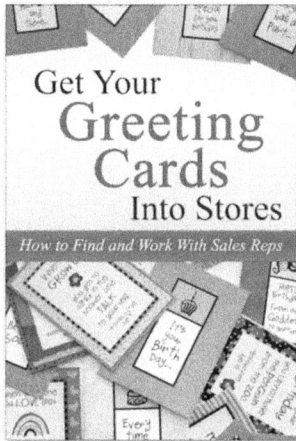

Get Your Greeting Cards into Stores

This book explains how to sell cards nationwide.
Included are detailed guidelines on: How to price cards for a profit,
get professional feedback, find sales representatives
and follow industry standards.

Information is also applicable to gift items, magnets, journals,
calendars, collectibles, etc.

20 Steps to Art Licensing

This is a book about how to license your art to companies
that publish greeting cards, or manufacture coffee mugs, magnets,
wall hangings, kitchen items, and dozens of other gift items.

Learn how to prepare your art, what companies to contact,
how to find agents, and what trade shows to attend. Includes extensive
resources on social media, copyrights, licensing community groups,
and lists of interviews with professional designers

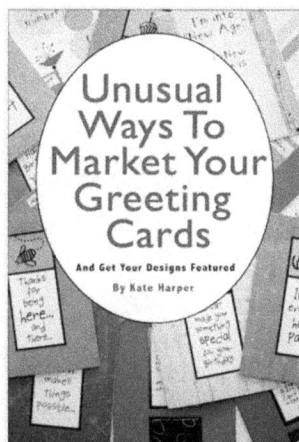

Unusual Ways to Market Greeting Cards

This booklet covers how to get your cards noticed
in non-traditional ways. Everything from why you should send cards
to your dentist, to how to get a special feature in national publications.

Great tips for designers who are starting out and want to
get their cards into the hands of people beyond friends and family.
Special Section: 22 Gift Industry Trade Publications
who seek out new greeting card designs and feature artists for free.

7 Mistakes Greeting Card Writers Make

This booklet explains what to avoid when submitting greeting card
verse to publishers. Learn how to create a trendy card that reflects
the contemporary world we live in, and how to use your own personal
experience to create card verse.

Topics include: How to avoid limiting your market, when to use
adjectives, not creating cards for enemies, write like people talk,
and why submissions are rejected. You can increase your odds of
success by 60% just by doing a few simple things.
Includes a list of card publishers, guidelines, links to writer interviews,
and writing exercises for creating good verse.

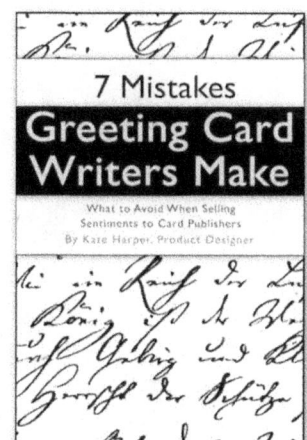

North Berkeley Press

www.kateharperdesigns.com

Online Class

Getting Into The Greeting Card Business

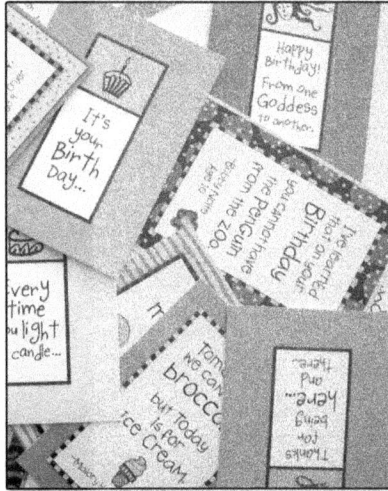

Getting into the Greeting Card Business is an online course hosted by the Skillshare, the educational website.

Whether you want to get your cards into stores, sell online, license your designs to card publishers, or work at a publisher, this course will cover the basic information on the greeting card business.

The information is based of Kate Harper's experience of working in the card industry for over 20 years in manufacturing and licensing.

Topics Covered:

- Fundamentals of card design
- How to transform art into a greeting card format
- How to write sentiments
- Make designs "market-ready" for industry standards
- Learn about top selling occasions
- Turn one card into a larger "collection"
- Make a card out of any image
- The handmade card business
- Where and how to sell cards (including online)
- Licensing art on cards
- Manufacturing and national distribution.

Register: http://skl.sh/1SfBXXp

When: You can sign up anytime. It is self-paced and has community support.

SKILLSHARE

https://www.skillshare.com/

North Berkeley Press

www.kateharperdesigns.com

www.ingramcontent.com/pod-product-compliance
Lightning Source LLC
Chambersburg PA
CBHW080216040426

42331CB00035B/3024